CLARKE GABLE
IN HIS OWN WORDS

CLARKE GABLE
IN HIS OWN WORDS

Compiled by Neil Grant

HAMLYN

ART EDITOR: ROBIN WHITECROSS
RESEARCH BY MARGARET WOMERSLEY
PRODUCTION: ALISON MYER
PICTURE RESEARCH: EMILY HEDGES & ANNA SMITH
EDITOR: SIAN FACER

THIS EDITION PUBLISHED IN 1992 BY PAUL HAMLYN PUBLISHING LIMITED,
PART OF REED INTERNATIONAL BOOKS LIMITED,
MICHELIN HOUSE, 81 FULHAM ROAD, LONDON SW3 6RB

A CATALOGUE RECORD FOR THIS BOOK IS AVAILABLE FROM THE BRITISH LIBRARY

ISBN 0 600 57458 X

PRODUCED BY MANDARIN OFFSET - PRINTED IN HONG KONG

CONTENTS

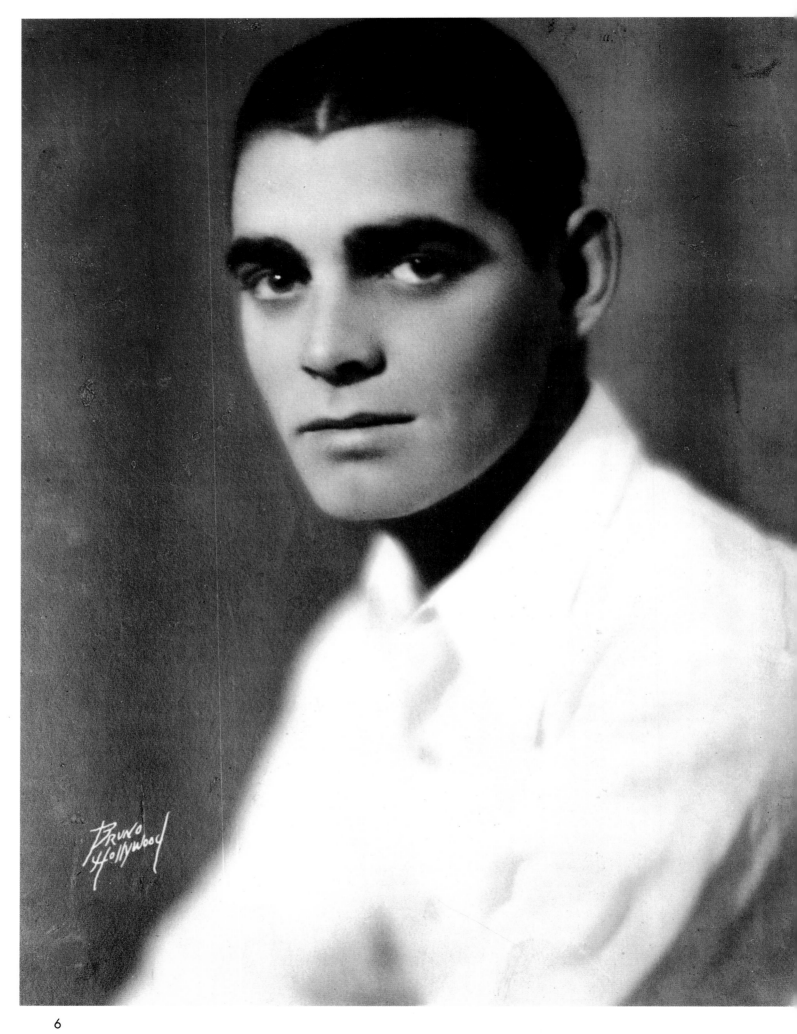

Bruno Hollywood

6

THE EASIEST WAY

"I towered over the other kids on the school bus,
hated doing homework, and
dreaded coming back to the farm"

William Clark Gable, known to childhood friends as Billy, was born and reared in a small town in Ohio, in the first year of the century. His father was a small farmer and one-time oil-worker. His mother, who also came from farming stock, was frail, and died when the baby was eight months old. Looked after by relatives for over a year, he returned home when his father was married again, to Jennie Dunlap, a dressmaker. It was a fortunate move for the young Gable. His relations with his father were to be troubled, but his stepmother adored him – and was adored by him. His need for a substitute-mother figure did not vanish when he grew up.

Childhood was ordinary enough. He was no great shakes with the books, and never graduated from high school, though he was useful on the baseball diamond. Girlfriends complained, as studio bosses were to do later, of his large, jug-handle ears. At sixteen he left home and took a job in the Firestone rubber factory in Akron, Ohio. A grim job it was by his account, even worse than the farm. He met a few music-hall actors and, impressed by the apparent glamor of their existence, decided to have a stab at it himself. His first theater job, in a local stock company, was unpaid and consisted in the main of running errands.

After the death of his stepmother, he went with his father to oil-booming Oklahoma, working a twelve-hour shift for a dollar a day. This had little appeal and at the age of twenty-one he left home for good, after a row with his father who thought all actors were fairies.

Acting jobs were hard to come by. In between spells working in a lumber camp and a department store, he was employed in a Kansas City stock company and, in the summer of 1922, by an equally indigent company in Oregon, where he began to get decent parts. No one thought he had much talent, but he met a drama coach and former Broadway actress, Josephine Dillon, who helped him enormously. Among other things, she is said to have been responsible for his characteristic gruff

"I respected my father and wanted his blessing.
It was Jennie who convinced him to let me go in peace. If it hadn't
been for her, I'd probably still be pitching hay in Ohio"

ON LEAVING HOME

delivery. She was fourteen years older than he, and presumably he was first attracted by what she could do for him. Love bloomed later and he married her in Los Angeles in December 1924.

So then, encouraged by Josephine Dillon, Clark Gable (She had also banished the 'Billy') began to make the rounds of the film studios. His first job, as an extra, was in *Forbidden Paradise*. Otherwise he had little luck. The smoothly seductive Valentino or John Gilbert type was then the fashion in male stars. Gable, with his big ears, large hands (as he admitted, like bunches of bananas), bad teeth and rough-hewn personality hardly fitted the image. However, some leading ladies found him attractive enough off-screen, and Gable attempted to advance his career by this variant of the studio-couch scenario. His marriage broke down as a result, and a wealthy, thrice-married socialite, Ria Langham, who was even older than his first wife, became his second.

With Ria now more or less in control, Gable accompanied her to New York in 1928, and through her gained a couple of good parts. Unfortunately the plays were less good, and quickly folded. He returned to Los Angeles in

1930 where Ria's promise of investment in the production gained him the leading role in the West Coast production of *The Last Mile*, a play which had been the making of Spencer Tracy, a future drinking partner.

The role produced the same effect for Gable. Lionel Barrymore was impressed by his performance (he was not alone) and arranged a screen test. MGM boss Irving Thalberg hated it, but agents were now interested in Gable, and he got a part in a William Boyd Western, *The Painted Desert*, after concealing his inability to ride a horse. A screen test for Warner Brothers was as disastrous as the first, but Barrymore hadn't given up and arranged a second test at MGM. Gable was signed up at $350 a week.

He played a succession of minor roles, nearly always as a heavy, mainly because the studio did not know what to do with him. A brief volcanic affair with Joan Crawford did his career no harm, and by *Night Nurse* (one of a dozen films he made in l931), he was secure in his attractive tough-guy image. Hitting Norma Shearer in *A Free Soul* epitomised the break with the smooth and gallant heroes of the previous generation.

"I had told him I didn't want to work in the oil fields, nohow.
I wanted to be an actor. Period. So he ups and
threatens me. I figured that was a good time to leave – quick.
So Dad and I parted not too friendly"

ON HIS FATHER

"I did a little bit of everything for ten dollars a week:
played the French horn in the orchestra,
hawked plays dressed as a clown on street corners,
and occasionally had a chance to act.
That's what they called it"

IN REPERTORY THEATER

"I make the audience laugh instead of cry... know what I mean?
I bump into props when I should be picking them up"

9

"Definitely there was no future for me in Hollywood.

I was no Valentino or Gilbert.

I was somewhat of a roughneck"

"I was pretty sore because they insisted on taping my big ears back.

One day, in a scene with Garbo, the tape snapped loose

and one ear flapped in the breeze.

That was the end of the taping"

DURING THE FILMING OF *SUSAN LENNOX* [1932]

"I always look twice at girls who are alive, vital,
alert, on their toes. The weeping-willow type,
the languidly drooping ladies never did appeal to me.
The first woman I ever really fell for — I was about twenty
at the time and she was around forty-five — was one of
the most vivid, energetic women I've ever known."

"I'd come home and she would start teaching.
I wasn't walking right, I wasn't breathing deeply, or
I entered the kitchen all wrong, my voice was too high.
She never did anything but teach, teach, teach!"

ON FIRST WIFE JOSEPHINE DILLON

"Ria is a woman who has been about,

she knows the world and life and how to handle men.

She has never been on the set with me once.

How about that for a good wife?"

ON RIA LANGHAM, SECOND WIFE

"I'm acting strictly for the money. I don't want to be very rich

but I don't want to give up what I've got"

"My God, she is a major star!

She knows everything there is to know about making movies.

I'll feel like a jerk and probably act like one too"

ON JOAN CRAWFORD

"Take Jane Russell, she was there, all of her.

*Whatever I held, she was **all** there.*

Like the old man said, 'I get my thrills that way'"

"They're all beautiful and I've had every one of them"

ON A PHOTO OF MGM LEADING LADIES

18

GOING WITH THE WIND

*"I know my limitations,
and I really am at my best in an open shirt,
blue jeans and boots"*

Making movies at such a rate, Gable was a big star – not the biggest but in the top ten – in less than three years. His early films were mostly run-of-the-mill Hollywood fare of the Thirties, but an exception might be made for *Red Dust* (1932), in which he played a rugged rubber plantation boss caught up in a romantic triangle with Mary Astor and Jean Harlow.

Even Gable was not immune to the usual studio grooming process. They gave up on his ears, but extracted his teeth and fitted him with dentures. He was less displeased with the studio publicity, which plugged him as a rugged, outdoors, hunting and fishing type, close enough to reality.

According to friends and colleagues, at this stage he remained very insecure, and retained some of the prejudices of the Ohio farmboy, he had once been gaining a – probably undeserved – reputation for having short arms and deep pockets. He liked to keep his cash about him. According to his friend and secretary

Jean Garceau, he was reluctant to invest it and would cruise around Hollywood with $3,000 in his wallet. He regarded his new wealth and popularity with caution.

Like several other of MGM's big stars, Gable crowned his reputation with a film for another studio, Columbia, to which he had been lent as a punishment for being difficult (rejecting scripts and demanding more money). The film was *It Happened One Night*, with Claudette Colbert. Gable, playing a tough-egg reporter, won an Oscar. (It was to be his only one.) This was also the film which, according to legend, ruined underwear manufacturers by revealing, when the star stripped off his shirt, that he wore no undershirt.

Among Gable's seventy-odd films, there are only a handful that critics would class as memorable, but most of the best were made in this period – the late 1930s. After *It Happened One Night* (1934) came *Mutiny on the Bounty* (1935), *San Francisco* (1936), and finally *Gone*

"They see me as an ordinary guy,
like a construction worker
or the guy who delivers your piano..."

With the Wind (1939). Gable was not obvious casting for Rhett Butler. He had serious misgivings about the part himself, and whenhe was first approached turned it down. Pressure was brought to bear: at the time Gable's emotional entanglements - married to Ria Langham, living with Carole Lombard – were causing him financial difficulties which meant he was in no position to buck the studio. There were more difficulties when filming started.

Gable did not get on with the director, George Cukor, and after boycotting the set for several days, succeeded in having him replaced with his own nominee, Victor Fleming.

The reason that Gable gained the Rhett Butler role was simply that it was the best role going that year and he was the most popular Hollywood leading man. His title as the 'King' of Hollywood had been officially bestowed through a publicity stunt in 1938 when Ed Sullivan, then a nationally syndicated movie columnist, asked his readers to elect both a 'king' and a 'queen' of Hollywood. Allegedly, 20 million votes were cast and Gable got most of them (Myrna Loy was voted 'queen'). He was officially crowned with a tin crown in an NBC radio broadcast, and the title, like John Wayne's 'Duke', was pinned on him for good. Unlike many previous Hollywood heroes, Gable was a man's man as well as a ladies' man.

It wasn't that he was discourteous to women, despite the famous slap of Norma Shearer. On the contrary he was gallant and considerate, though also dominant. Men liked to identify with him no less than women liked to imagine being seduced by him.

As with all great stars, it was his own personality, added to modest but genuine histrionic ability, that explained his huge popularity with the fans. Besides his affable, thoroughly masculine charm, he conveyed an honourable toughness and a kind of natural dignity of the kind that protects a man from ever making a fool of himself.

"I worked three months straight [filming] without a day off.
If this is what it's like being a success,
when will I have a chance to enjoy it?"

"I'm tired and have nothing to show for it.
Nothing different than working on the farm – up before dawn
and home after dark.
But MGM's making hay, not me!"

"Every actor should work with Garbo.
She gets what she wants – in fact, she walked off the set six times
because she didn't like the script.
And she went home every day at five regardless
of what was going on. It was in her contract.
I filed that away until the time came when I could have the same
clause in my agreement"

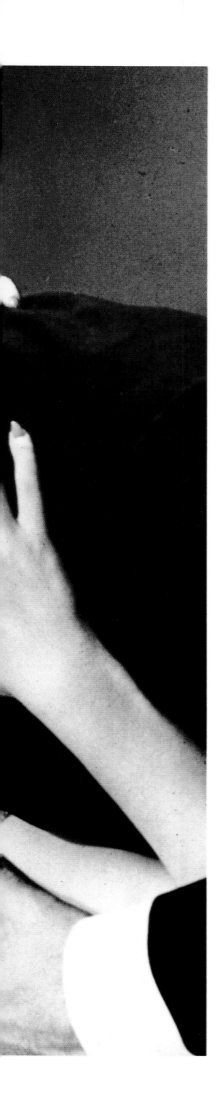

"It's a chain of accidents.
When you step into Hollywood, you wind
yourself into thousands of chains of accidents.
If all of the thousands happen to come out
exactly right – and the chance of that figures
out to be one in eight million –
then you'll be a star"

"Every time they say 'Cut!'
and it's the last take of a movie,
I feel I'll never be hired for another one...
All actors feel they're not entitled to happiness
and all that money, that some evil god
will take it away from us when we get it"

"This 'King' stuff is pure bullshit.

I eat and sleep and go to the bathroom just like everyone else.

There's no special light that shines inside me and makes me a star.

I'm just a lucky slob from Ohio.

"The guy is good.

There's nobody in the business who can touch him

and you're a fool to try. And the bastard knows it,

so don't fall for that humble stuff"

ON SPENCER TRACY

"I just work here.
I try to work well and hard.
They have an investment
in me. They've spent money
on me. It's my business
to work, not to think"

"The character is a pansy.
And I'm not going to
be seen wearing a pigtail
and knickers"

AS FLETCHER CHRISTIAN IN MUTINY ON THE BOUNTY

"I'm still going to wear the same size hat"

After winning an Oscar

"The only reason [the fans] come to see me

is that I know life is great

and they know I know it"

*"I didn't want the part
and told David [Selznick] that...
Selznick wouldn't take no
for an answer"*

*"There are going to be six million
eyes on me all daring me to fail"*

*"Miss Leigh makes Scarlett so
vividly lifelike that it makes my
playing of Rhett much simpler
than I had expected"*

*"I'm sick and tired of this Rhett
business"*

*"If it hadn't been for that damn
picture, nobody would want me
any more. In fact they wouldn't
even remember who I was"*

ON GONE WITH THE WIND

STRANGE INTERLUDE

*"If anything happens to me,
don't let them make a circus out of it"*

In August 1942 Gable joined the U.S. Air Force, volunteering for combat duties. It was a surprising decision. In the first place, although very fit, he was forty-one years old, a shade elderly for a warrior. Moreover, most Hollywood stars took the view that they could do more for the war effort by charity appearances and publicity. Victor Fleming, who had directed *Gone With the Wind* and who wanted Gable to make a film about the flying ace, Eddie Rickenbacker, asked, 'How can that guy make better use of himself: by trying to do something any healthy twenty-year-old can do better or by telling the story of our greatest fighting flyer?' At the same time, Fleming recognized that in another sense Gable had done the 'right' thing, which in the long run would do his career no harm either. 'He will be a bigger American legend than Paul Bunyan and all the rest of them combined. He's the representative man of our time. No one will ever forget him.'

Gable's own motive was largely simple patriotism, but what made his decision certain was his desolation after the death of his third wife, Carole Lombard who, moreover, had urged him to enlist before she was killed in a plane crash in January 1942. Additionally, perhaps, Gable's decision to join up was spurred by his unconscious instinct to live up to a popular image of the kind that Fleming, with pardonable exaggeration, postulated. It was somehow in his nature always to be the kind of figure the public admired.

He entered the service as an enlisted man, but soon graduated from an officers' school

"I'm going to enlist in the Air Corps,
but not until I get my head together and sort things out.
I don't expect to come back
and I don't want to come back"

near Miami. He trained as a gunner and flew with 351 Bomber Group in England as a photographer, winning two military awards.

There are always difficulties when a celebrity joins the forces – the Germans were anxious to catch him and put a price of $5,000 on his head – but Gable apparently neither sought nor received special treatment.

Gable was not the same man when he returned from the war – older, more cynical, to an extent disillusioned. How much the change was due to his war experience and how much to the loss of Lombard, whose photo he carried in a hinged attachment to his service dog-tag throughout the war, no one can estimate. He certainly had less time for the frivolities of Hollywood. Never allowing his sense of his own identity to be swamped by the media image, he was irritated when, as an undoubtedly middle-aged man, he was cast as the lover of actresses young enough to be his daughters.

Apart from *The Hucksters* and maybe one or two others, his films in the Forties and Fifties were fairly undistinguished. Gable, though never an alcoholic nor a lecher, also drank a good deal too much and slept with too many women.

"Look at the King, the King of Hollywood!

Sure looks like the Jack now, doesn't he?"

REMOVING HIS FALSE TEETH WHILE WASHING UP WITH FELLOW ROOKIES

"If I ever fall into Hitler's hands,
the sonovabitch will put me in a cage like a big gorilla.
He'd exhibit me all over Germany"

"I saw so much in the way of death and destruction that
I realized that I hadn't been singled out for grief —
that others were suffering and losing their loved ones
just as I lost Ma "

ON CAROLE LOMBARD

*"Well, we've won the war
and there's peace now everywhere.
Everywhere except here in Hollywood, where
the fighting for good scripts, good
billing and good dressing rooms never ends"*

TO PLEASE A LADY

"That's what's so strange about life.
The brave ones don't make it..."

ON WIVES AND WOMEN

In 1939, during a two-day pause in filming *Gone With the Wind*, Gable married the love of his life, Carole Lombard. In marked contrast to his first two wives, she was considerably younger than he. An attractive, humorous and very lively blonde, she was given to practical jokes, blunt speaking and blue language, and was regarded by the more starchy denizens of Hollywood as a little too outrageous. They bought a ranch in the San Fernando valley, went duck-shooting together, named their home House of Two Gables, and called each other 'Ma' and 'Pa'.

They were married less than three years (though they had been living together for some time before that), and cynics might suppose that only Lombard's sad death prevented the marriage going the way of most Hollywood marriages, sooner or later. But it does seem to have been a remarkable success, and several of Gable's closest friends recorded their opinion that he never really got over Carole's death early in 1942 – when the plane taking her on a government-sponsored tour to sell war bonds crashed in Arizona.

Gable was not a great lover. Carole Lombard said he was the worst lay she ever had, though that was just an expression of her desire to provoke – not that Gable himself could be provoked by such means. He did, on the other hand, have a lot of women. He was married five times, he had several passionate affairs, and a vast number of one-night-stands. No doubt he slept with some women out of sheer self-defense.

After the war, still missing Carole and feeling unwilling to commit himself to anyone else, he led a wild bachelor's life for a time. He

43

"Did you ever see anyone more beautiful?
There was never a person in this world who was so generous,
so full of fun. God damn it, why Ma?"

"Personality would be a thousand times,
ten thousand times, more important to me "

went out with an actress named Virginia Gray, whom he'd known for years, and even proposed to her once, only to run the next day.

When he did marry again, he made an odd choice – an English socialite with three previous husbands including Douglas Fairbanks Sr and a titled gent from whom she had appropriated her own title, 'Lady Ashley'. It seems they met at a party in December 1949 and got on well, but the marriage lasted just a year.

His fifth and last wife was an ex-actress called Kay, or Kathleen, Spreckels. Several people commented on her resemblance to Lombard, and he had known her for some time before he married her in 1955. This marriage too was a success, and eventually Kay became pregnant. Gable had no children by then, and welcomed the prospect, but his son by Kay was not born until the spring of 1961, and by that time the King was dead.

*"After we got married, I asked her what she wanted
more than anything. We were looking over the property,
and she said, 'I'd like manure for the bottom thirty.'
She meant it too"*

*"Sometimes I wonder how she'd take things the way they are today,
and I always come up with the same answer - with a laugh.
She'd get through it better than me"*

ON CAROLE LOMBARD

"When it's over, it's over.
No questions, no tears, no farewell kisses"
EXPLAINING PREFERENCE FOR BROTHELS

"Because I can pay them to go away.
The others stay around, want a big romance,
movie lovemaking.
I'm not the world's greatest lover...
With one of these floozies,
I don't have to pretend that I'm Clark Gable"
ASKED WHY HE LIKED PROSTITUTES

"She makes no trouble.
Sometimes the homely ones are the best kind,
easy to please
and very grateful afterward"
ASKED WHY HE WENT OUT WITH A VERY PLAIN WOMAN ON AN ARMY BASE, 1942

"To tell you the truth, women scare me..."

"Looks and age don't cut any ice with me.
They're not important.
I've always leaned towards the medium in height and size.
However, if the right girl happens to be short
and round or tall and thin,
I suppose I'll think she's perfect"

"I certainly don't like ultra-spectacular women,
the ones who go in for startling make-up and clothes.
I like the girls who look conservatively smart with a smooth finish.
No straggling hair or run-over heels or missing buttons"

"I've never believed in that bunk about a man's ideal girl.
I've probably had a dozen ideals in my life,
each one being the person
I happened to be in love with at the time"

"I'm a very happy man.
What can I say about Kay.
She's a wonderful woman and a perfect companion"
ON HIS FIFTH MARRIAGE

"Old Kathleen has an awful lot of remarkable stuff in her.
A lot of good plain horse-sense.
She can do anything"
KATHLEEN SPRECKELS, FIFTH WIFE

"When Kay gets ill I panic inside.
She's the best thing besides Carole
that ever happened to me"

THE MAN AND THE MISFITS

"On my tombstone they should write,

'He was lucky and he knew it'"

Gable was the ideal Hollywood star. He knew what was wanted from him and he did it. Unlike his co-stars in *The Misfits*, he was not neurotic, and he never suffered from the megalomania that is an occupational disease of film stars and pop idols. The appalling pressures of the studio system he shrugged off. Although he had quarrels with the studio, and with individuals – and he derived a good deal of satisfaction from rejecting MGM's attempt to rehire him after it had unilaterally terminated his contract in 1954 – he never seriously challenged the system. The studio meanly refused to give him a percentage of the profits on his films, including *Gone With the Wind*, which would have made him a very rich man, but his popularity was such that he was never out of work, and never had to worry about waning success or a waning bank balance. He belonged to that group of Hollywood stars – Cooper, Stewart, Fonda & Co. – who never went (and still haven't gone) out of fashion. The Gable character, even in the most humdrum movies, still holds up.

And the later films, on the whole, were pretty humdrum, though usually watchable and, in some cases, very successful at the box office. In 1952 he made his one British film, *Never Let Me Go*, then took off for East Africa for *Mogambo*, a remake of his early success, *Red Dust*, with Ava Gardner and Grace Kelly replacing Jean Harlow and Mary Astor. Gable took more than a shine to Grace Kelly, but she was twenty-three and he was fifty-one.

Before *Mogambo* was released, MGM announced that it would not be renewing Gable's contract the following year. Like all the big studios, MGM was finding life harder, with television – a medium that

"I did all the wrong things...
The worst was not getting a percentage of
'Gone with the Wind'"

never attracted Gable – chopping into audience figures. Most of Gable's associates at the studio had passed on or been kicked out, and he didn't care for the new generation.

When the receipts started rolling in from *Mogambo*, the studio changed its mind, but Gable, incensed, wasn't going back. He made his last nine pictures as a freelance, and on a percentage, although it was only for the last, *The Misfits*, that he was paid the kind of fee that today's entertainers would consider normal.

These were better years, with Gable enjoying a real family life (Kay Williams had two children from a previous marriage) at the ranch, though Kay's poor health, following a miscarriage in 1955, caused him intense anxiety. He made a routine western, *The Tall Men*, a romantic comedy (at the age of fifty-four) with Doris Day, *Teacher's Pet*, and a tense submarine drama, *Run Silent Run Deep* (1958). What critics regard as one of his best films, was his last.

Gable had profound misgivings about the part of the redundant cowboy in *The Misfits*, and asked for a huge fee of $1 million on the assumption that he would be turned down. He was not, and the film went ahead, directed by John Huston and co-starring Marilyn Monroe and Montgomery Clift, it was made mostly on location in the desert, with Gable, who never liked to employ a stunt man, roping wild horses and being dragged by a truck in the hot dust, or waiting for someone to fix the continual crises caused by the neuroses of his co-stars (in particular the fast-collapsing marriage of Monroe and scriptwriter Arthur Miller).

The Misfits brought Gable the best reviews he'd ever had. The fact is he had never given a bad performance for nearly 30 years, and maybe the critics were not entirely unmoved by sentiment.

For the King never read the reviews. He died of a heart attack a few weeks after the end of filming, on November 16, 1960.

"My days of playing the dashing young lover are over.
I'm no longer believable in those parts.
There has been considerable talk about older guys wooing
and winning leading ladies half their age.
I don't think the public likes it, and I don't care for it myself.
It's not realistic. The actresses I started out with have long since
quit playing glamor girls and sweet young things
Now it's time I acted my age" 1959

"See how high you can get those sons of bitches to go.
When you get their very best offer, tell them to take all the money,
their studio, their cameras and lighting equipment,
and shove it all up their ass"
TO HIS AGENT, WHEN **MGM** TRIED TO REHIRE HIM

*"The public came to the movies
to see Gable as Gable.
They don't want to see me
pulling any tricks and
getting serious on 'em.
Besides, I'm too old to change"*
CONTEMPLATING HIS PART IN THE MISFITS

*"They're all nuts. Monroe is
never on time if she shows up at
all. No one else gets here on
time. We don't start shooting
until afternoon but, goddam it,
I leave at five and that's it!"*

*"The title sums up this mess.
Miller, Monroe and Clift —
they don't know what the hell
they're doing.
We don't belong in the same
room together. "*
THE MISFITS

"I like the idea of acting my age... If it comes off, and I think it will,
I'll go right ahead playing the same type of guy.
I have no idea if I can attain the success as a character actor as I did
playing the dashing young lover – it's a chance I have to take.
Not everyone is able to do it"

"I'm taking time off until the baby is born.

No more pictures now.

I want to be there at home and

I want to be there a good many months afterward..."

ON COMPLETING *THE MISFITS*

PICTURE CREDITS

PAGE 1: A film with drama, romance and comedy. Clark Gable stars with his wife Carole Lombard in *No Man Of Her Own* (Paramount, 1932). KOBAL COLLECTION.

Page 2: Starring with Vivien Leigh and Olivia de Havilland, Clark Gable in *Gone With The Wind* (MGM, 1939). SNAP PHOTOS/KATZ PICTURES.

PAGE 6: At 24, Clark Gable was performing in a travelling company. KOBAL COLLECTION.

PAGE 7: 1903 and 'Billy' was 18 months old, born in Cadiz, Ohio. SNAP PHOTOS/KATZ PICTURES.

PAGE 8: Clark, the farm boy. KOBAL COLLECTION.

PAGE 9 The cast of *Hawk Island* captivated by Gable's discovery. KOBAL COLLECTION.

PAGE 10: Clark with Norma Shearer in *A Free Soul* (MGM, 1931). The film demanded heavy melodrama and outdated attitudes but they gave an impressive performance. SNAP PHOTOS/KATZ PICTURES.

PAGE 11: Starring in *The Easiest Way* one of Gable's first films, featured here with Anita Page. SNAP PHOTOS/KATZ PICTURES.

PAGE 12 A relaxed portrait of Clark Gable, without his ears taped back for filming. KOBAL COLLECTION.

PAGE 13: Clark Gable talking to a fashion model, Elizabeth Allen. KOBAL COLLECTION.

PAGE 14: Clark with his second wife Ria Langham and Norma Shearer. KOBAL COLLECTION.

PAGE 15: A typical portrait of Clark Gable nearing the height of his fame. KOBAL COLLECTION.

PAGE 16: Starring opposite Joan Crawford in *Possessed* (MGM, 1931). SNAP PHOTOS/KATZ PICTURES.

PAGE 17: Clark Gable and again Joan Crawford starring in *Chained* (MGM, 1934). Clark treated her with great respect as an actress and was captivated by her. SNAP PHOTOS/KATZ PICTURES.

PAGE 18: Now with a moustache, Clark Gable was rated one of the top ten in America. He was given the image of a 'rugged, outdoors' type which displeased him. KOBAL COLLECTION.

PAGE 19: Clark and Myrna Loy, voted king and queen of the movies in 1936, star in *Too Hot To Handle* (MGM, 1938). LONDON FEATURES INTERNATIONAL.

PAGE 20: With Jean Harlow. It was thanks to actors like Gable and Spencer Tracy that she achieved stardom. SNAP PHOTOS/KATZ PICTURES.

PAGE 21: With Loretta Young in *Call Of The Wild* (Twentieth Century, 1935). SNAP PHOTOS/KATZ PICTURES.

PAGE 22: Gable starring in *Susan Lennox – Her Rise And Fall* with Greta Garbo (MGM, 1931). SNAP PHOTOS/KATZ PICTURES.

PAGE 23: An MGM studio portrait of Clark, 1931-2. SNAP PHOTOS/KATZ PICTURES.

PAGE 24-5: Jean Harlow and Clark Gable star in *Saratoga*. Not the greatest of Gable's films and Harlow's last. KOBAL COLLECTION.

PAGE 26: Now seen as a symbol of virility and sex appeal, Clark in an MGM studio portrait. SNAP PHOTOS/KATZ PICTURES.

PAGE 27: Clark Gable and Spencer Tracy star in *Boomtown* (MGM, 1940). SNAP PHOTOS/KATZ PICTURES.

PAGE 28 *Mutiny On The Bounty*, a film which is possibly one of his greatest, received high honours among the critics. Snap Photos/Katz Pictures.

PAGE 30 As an Oscar winner for *It Happened One Night*, Clark Gable became complacent. SNAP PHOTOS/KATZ PICTURES.

PAGE 31 A studio portrait of Clark at MGM studios in 1936. SNAP PHOTOS/KATZ PICTURES.

PAGE 32 Notably one of Clark Gable's greatest performances with co-star Vivien Leigh. SNAP PHOTOS/KATZ PICTURES.

PAGE 34: Pictured here is Captain C. Gable of the U.S. Air Force, enlisting as a photographer and winning two military awards. SNAP PHOTOS/KATZ PICTURES.

PAGE 35: He did 'The Right Thing' by joining the forces and didn't regret it. KOBAL COLLECTION.

PAGE 36: Clark was a great socialiser and heavy drinker but never an alcoholic. KOBAL COLLECTION.

PAGE 37: *Too Hot To Handle* (MGM, 1938), an excellent performance by Clark Gable. SNAP PHOTOS/KATZ PICTURES.

PAGE 38: Middle-aged when he returned from the war, Clark was still cast opposite young female stars. KOBAL COLLECTION.

PAGE 39: Irene Dunne is here christening the *SS Carole Lombard* with Clark in the background. SNAP PHOTOS/KATZ PICTURES.

PAGE 40: After the worries of war, age begins to show, but to his fans Gable is still 'King'. KOBAL COLLECTION.

PAGE 41: When returning to films Clark had less success and was fighting for good parts. KOBAL COLLECTION.

PAGE 42: Gable married Carole Lombard, the love of his life, and was devastated when she was killed in a plane crash. KOBAL COLLECTION.

PAGE 43: Starring in *No Man* with Carole Lombard. SNAP PHOTOS/KATZ PICTURES.

PAGE 44: Gable in *Too Hot To Handle* with Carole Lombard by his side visiting. SNAP PHOTOS/KATZ PICTURES.

PAGE 45: Clark Gable and his new wife Carole Lombard. KOBAL COLLECTION.

PAGE 46: Pure Gable. Working on the land. KOBAL COLLECTION.

PAGE 48: Ria Langham, Clark's second wife, with Clark Gable descending a train in 1931. SNAP PHOTOS/KATZ PICTURES.

PAGE 49: Clark with his fourth wife Sylvia Ashley. KOBAL COLLECTION.

PAGE 50: Clark Gable with his fifth and final wife, Kay Spreckels. KOBAL COLLECTION.

PAGE 51: Clark Gable and Kay. Kay bore him his first and only son, whom he was not destined to see. SNAP PHOTOS/KATZ PICTURES.

PAGE 52: Clark in *The Misfits* (United Artists, 1961). SNAP PHOTOS/KATZ PICTURES.

PAGE 53: Clark Gable again in *The Misfits* an ill-fated drama with Marilyn Monroe. KOBAL COLLECTION.

PAGE 54: *Mogambo*, his last film with MGM, in which he starred with Grace Kelly. SNAP PHOTOS/KATZ PICTURES.

PAGE 55 Clark Gable in the last years of his life. SNAP PHOTOS/KATZ PICTURES.

PAGE 56 Turning grey, Clark didn't have the same success in 1956 as in the 1930's. SNAP PHOTOS/KATZ PICTURES.

PAGE 57: Clark Gable in *Mogambo* (MGM, 1953), a flabby remake of *Red Dust*. KOBAL COLLECTION.

PAGE 58: Clark Gable and Marilyn Monroe in *The Misfits* (United Artists, 1961). A film 'wallowing in self-pity.' SNAP PHOTOS/KATZ PICTURES.

PAGE 60: Clark Gable sitting with Arthur Miller (Marilyn's husband) on the set of *The Misfits*. KOBAL COLLECTION.

PAGE 61 Clark Gable sitting on the set of *Across The Wide Missouri* (MGM, 1951), a Western not up to his best but still convincing. KOBAL COLLECTION.